Things They Don't Teach You in School

(but you should know when you get out on your own.)

Ron Dingee

ISBN: 150850329X
ISBN-13: 9781508503293:

DEDICATION

To my grand-children
B.J, and Melissa
Alex, Katie, and Vicky
and Isaac.

CONTENTS

ACKNOWLEDGMENTS

Anyone who attempts to write a book knows that the author is only a part of the process. First, he or she needs regular encouragement and patience from friends and family. Then, lots of help reading, re-reading, editing, and proofing the manuscript often with hundreds of suggested changes.

In the process of writing this book, I thank good friends, Sharon Whitaker, Lori Catlett, Nancy Hinz, Katherine Dingee, and my wife, Evelyn Dingee, for their reading, editing, proofing, and their persistent and loving encouragement.

Thank You

Chapter 1
The Real World Outside

Congratulations on your graduation from high school. You probably worked hard and earned good grades, but school teaches you the things you need to get a job, but not what you need to know to live on your own.

During the eight years between seventeen and twenty-five you will experience enormous changes. First, you will graduate high school, maybe go to college, leave home, and get a job. During this time you will be renting apartments, perhaps marrying and having kids, buying a home and cars, and will be buying insurance. You might be able to write an algorithm or project the trajectory of a rocket to the moon, but can you balance your checkbook? Do you know the difference between term and whole life insurance? Do you know how to negotiate the price of a car, or do you know the differences between a MMA and a MMF?

What follows is the accumulation of my knowledge, and many experiences over the past 75 years. I started putting this together several years ago after I became aware of how unprepared my own children were to face the real world beyond my doorstep when they left home.

The world is waiting for you with glee because you have needs and money, but not knowledge. Lessons will be very expensive and some unscrupulous people are out there just waiting to get what they can from you. There will be very few second chances.

First, I want to discuss what I consider to be the eight facts of life.

1.   Money makes the world go 'round, not love.

2. Each person has a recipe for success.
3. You can be anything you want to be.
4. There's no place for drugs or alcohol in life.
5. You are NOT an island.
6. Stuff happens
7. Learn the rules
8. The three F's in life

1. Money makes the world go 'round, not love: At this moment, as you are reading this, there are people meeting in smoke filled rooms for the sole purpose of coming up with new ideas to separate you from your money. These ideas range from legal to immoral.

Now, there are many, many honest, hard-working people doing their best to do their job, and if you treat them as though all people were thieves, they would be offended. Just be wary. And, when you find an honest one, make note and use their services again and again and recommend them to others. Then there are the industries who lie through their teeth to make a profit. Tobacco companies say that smoking doesn't cause cancer, and candy companies deny that sugar causes cavities. Follow the money!

2. Every person has a recipe for success: Everyone is filled with wants, desires, likes, dislikes, temptations, talents, knowledge, and experiences that make him or her uniquely prepared to be successful at something. There are some people who, at a very early age are inspired to their purpose in life. Take for example the 3 year old who hears a piano play and knows at that moment that they must become a concert pianist. Or, take the young child who learns to ice skate at age 6 and is inspired to become an Olympic champion.

Others however may not get such obvious direction early in life and, rather than getting a single direction, may be blessed with many, many different talents and abilities. The bottom line is that there is a purpose for your life. Some find it early while others find it later.

3. You can be anything you want: In this country you can go, do, have, or be anything you want!!! There are very few excuses why you can't. There are three conditions however: You must want it, you must be willing to work for it, and three... be willing to pay the price.

Sometimes the price is money, sometimes it is time, sometimes labor. Most often, it is a combination of all three.

There are of course some realities… If you are only 5 ft tall, you can't be an NBA player and yes, your parents divorced, or a parent died, or you were mistreated. Maybe you are poor or your parents were drug/alcohol users. Still, no excuse. Everyone has a story. There have been many studies of twins where both kids had the same disadvantages, but one excelled in life while the other failed. Why?

4. No drugs or alcohol: Alcohol and drugs have absolutely no place in your life. There is positively no compromise on this issue. You must function at 100% all the time to keep a job and a family. If not, there are thousands of people ready to step in to take your place.

5. You are NOT an island: You do not have the right to do what you want with your life. You are not living alone on an island. How many times have I heard kids say, "Leave me alone. Mind your own business. It's my life." We all have associations with family, friends, co-workers, and neighbors. If you smoke, it will be a loved one who will watch you slowly die from lung cancer and miss you when gone.

6. Stuff happens: I strongly urge you to have a clean, honest, moral life with a good education and   planning. But, things happen… they just happen. You can get struck with cancer, have an auto accident, experience a heart attack, endure floods, or be in the path of a tornado, etc… things just happen. But, if you walk too close to the back of a cow, you're more likely to step into something than someone who doesn't.

7. Learn the Rules: Become affiliated with a church, synagogue, or temple. Everyone needs a moral compass … something that points you in the right direction especially in difficult times. You need to have some rules, some guidelines. Every game has their fair and foul lines. Life is the same. Get to know the rules and know who is and isn't playing by them.

8.   **The three F's in life:** Faith, Family, and Friends. Don't forget them. They are the most important things in your life.

Lastly, ever notice that Home Depot is often located close to Lowe's? How about McDonald's, Wendy's, and many other fast food chains? Why do they think they can compete among their competitors? It's because they all believe that they know who they are and have something different to offer. Most major, successful companies have written vision statements of who they are and who they serve.

People should be the same. Who are you, what are you, and what do you stand for? Are you the person who takes or the one who gives? Do you do the least just to get by, or do you try your best? Are you honest or dishonest? Make up your mind... what kind of person do you want to be.

Chapter 2
Banking

Most people forget that banks are a business. They exist to make money just like any other business except their product is money not clothes, tools, or sporting goods.

There are many kinds of banks: State Banks, Federal Banks, Commercial Banks, Savings Banks, Mercantile Banks, Farmer's Banks, and Local Banks just to name a few. Don't forget credit unions. In most cases they are regulated by Federal and State laws. There are different kinds of institutions to serve different financial needs. It pays to shop around.

While banks and credit unions are both financial institutions that offer similar services (checking and savings accounts, auto loans, and mortgages, etc.), the main difference between a bank and a credit union is that "customers" of a credit union are members, and they own the institution. A **bank** is a company, and like most companies, a bank aims to maximize profits for its shareholders. A **credit union** is a cooperative and is often a not-for-profit institution that is owned by its members (customers) who democratically elect a board of directors. Credit unions tend to focus on members' needs and attempt to provide credit at reasonable rates. There are pros and cons to participating in either financial institution.

Whichever bank or credit union you decide to do business with, make certain it is federally insured to protect you against loss. With banks this is FDIC. With credit unions it is usually NCUA. I know, at this stage, you probably don't have enough money to worry about, but you could hit the lottery or inherit from your grand-parents.

FDIC (Federal Deposit Insurance Corp.) is an independent agency of the federal government. It was created in 1933 in response to the thousands of bank failures that occurred in the 1920s and early 1930s. Since the start of FDIC insurance on January 1, 1934, no depositor has lost a single cent of insured funds as a result of a failure.

Similar to FDIC, NCUA (The National Credit Union Administration) is also an independent federal agency created by the United States Congress to regulate, charter, and supervise federal credit unions.

Both FDIC and NCUA insure deposits of up to $250,000 per depositor. Now, if you have more than one account (checking, savings, CD's), the sum total is added together. However, if you have an account in your name, your wife's name, and both of your names together, you could, in effect, be protected up to $750,000.

Another thing... If you have an account in the Third Federal Bank on Main St. and another account in the Third Federal Bank on Center St., your insured amount is the total of your accounts in both banks.

Whoops, another thing... If the Anytown Savings and Loan is owned by the Third Federal Bank, again, the sum total of the value of the accounts in <u>both</u> banks are totaled together. So, when you have enough to worry about, be careful or you could lose your money, over $250,000, if the bank fails.

Banks often bundle their services together which may or may not include services you do not require so choosing a bank or credit union can be a challenging experience, but the time spent can save you a lot of money over the long term.

Now, with these lessons in mind let's discuss a few dealings you will have with banks. (A whole chapter is devoted to mortgages.) I will use the term "bank" to refer to both bank or credit union.

Checking Accounts

It used to be you could walk into a bank and say, "I want to open a checking or savings account" and be out in 10 minutes. Nowadays, it's a major ordeal. Not only do they have a dozen or more different plans for checking or savings accounts, but then you have thousands of check styles and colors to choose from.

To be fair, the reason why there are so many choices is because we all have different banking needs, and the bank has to have a way to charge for those individual services.

Things to consider when opening a checking account:

1. Do you need a minimum balance? How much?
2. How many checks do you write each month?
3. Do you need some kind of overdraft protection? In the event you write a check without adequate funds in the checking account, (called "bouncing a check") the money can be automatically withdrawn from your savings account, or the money can be taken from a preapproved line of credit. Avoid this kind of over draft privilege.
4. Do you need to make electronic transfers? Sometimes if you have more than one account, money can be transferred from one bank to another with or without charge.
5. How about automatic payments? If you have periodic recurring bills such as rent, utilities, insurance, etc., then you can have the bank pay these bills monthly, quarterly, or annually.
6. Do you have many other banking needs like Traveler's Checks, wire transfers, or automatic transfers from savings to checking? Banks can offer a package deal which include almost anything you can imagine, but watch out because you may be paying for services you may never need.
7. Do you want a credit or debit card associated with the account? More on plastic money later.
8. Can your everyday banking be done at ATM machines… without cost?
9. Can you do online banking?

Banks have different charges for different services. For example, some types of checking accounts advertise free checking, but charge you to purchase the book of checks whereas other banks charge a fixed fee per check when you write it. Other banks may have a monthly service charge whereas others may waive the service charge if you keep a minimum balance in your savings account. Some banks may pay you interest on any balance over a minimum balance in the checking account. So, as you can see, you need to evaluate your needs, do the math, and try to tailor the account you choose to suit your needs.

Unless you have a very good reason to do so, keeping more money in a checking account than you need to cover your day to day needs is a good waste of money since checking accounts pay very, very little interest, if any. It is best to keep the bulk of your money in some form of a savings account, MMA, or MMF. Again, more on this later.

OK, speaking of checks, what are all those numbers on the check? There are three that you should know about.

The first is of course the check number which is usually found in the upper right corner of the check. Down on the bottom left of the check is the bank tracking or routing number. This number is what you need if you transfer money from an account in another bank or investment company. It can also be needed if you set up automatic payments for a company. The last number, also on the bottom of the check, but in the middle, is your account number. Sometimes the check number will be repeated on the bottom right.

When writing the amount in the space provided, put your first number right up to the dollar sign so that there's no space to add another number like this $10.00 not $ 10.00. The same goes when you write in the amount. Make your first letter as far left as you can leaving no room for anything extra. If you make a small error, scratch it out and initial it, or start a new check if there's any question.

There are a couple of different ways to keep track of your balance. Checks come with three different methods for keeping track of your balance. Your three methods are:

1. The check has an NCR coating on the back which   transfers onto a page below.
2. There is a Check Register Book where you enter the check number, description, amount and new balance.
3. The check has s stub attached. You indicate the check info on the stub.

Personally, I like to use a money management software like Quicken.

IMPORANT: Use the Memo line to further detail the purpose of the check. If you pay your rent by check, indicate "Rent-May" in the Memo line. If you give someone money as a loan, be sure to write "Loan" on the Memo line.

Banks now make it possible to make deposits by just taking a picture of the check with your pad or smartphone, and you can pay bills using an online BillPay service, or send money using Pop Money. One problem with all of these modern services is that it is much harder to keep track of your balance if you pay recurring bills automatically, use a debit card at the store, the credit card at the gas station, and pay some bills with BillPay.

Savings

Savings accounts, like checking accounts, can be complicated. Banks offer several different kinds of savings accounts each having their own advantages & disadvantages.

1. Passbook Savings
This is the simplest way to secure your money, but not the best, because this account pays the lowest rate of interest. However, your money is always available and safe. These accounts are good for short

term savings where you expect to use the money soon or to accumulate money to put into a longer term account later.

2. Money Market Accounts (MMA's)

MMA's pay a higher rate of interest rate than Passbook accounts and you can write checks like a checking account. The difference is that you can write only a few checks per month and they must exceed $250.

3. Money Market Funds (MMF's)

Banks (and here I mean only banks) usually have investment services available which offer MMF's. MMF's usually pay a higher rate of interest than MMA's or Passbook Savings. You also need to find out if they are FDIC insured. MMF's are not considered to be 100% secured (how about 99.9%). You can also get MMF's through investment companies.

4. Certificates of Deposit (CD's)

CD's pay a higher rate of interest than Passbook accounts, but your money will be tied up for a specified period of time and you can't write checks. You can withdraw money from your CD before it matures, but you will pay a penalty which is usually six month's interest. CD's are a very conservative investment option. Usually, a five year CD pays a higher interest rate than a one year CD. To maximize your return, you can "ladder" your CD's. This means that you take out 5 CD's for 1-2-3-4-5 years and when the first one matures, it gets rolled over for five years.

If you were to win the lottery or a large inheritance, what do you do with your millions? You can deposit your money into a CDARS account with certain banks or investment companies. CDARS stands for, CD Account Registry Service. Since FDIC only guarantees your money up to $250,000, CDARS takes your millions and divides it up among many different banks that are FDIC insured. You can find a CDARS bank near you online.

To find banks with good interest rates, check out Bankrate.com, Maxmyinterest.com, and money-rates.com/cdrates.htm

I also recommend that you go to cfp.net or napfa.org for a fee only financial and insurance planner when you have money.

529 College Savings Plan The 529 Plan is a state, tax-advantaged investment plan designed to encourage saving for the future higher education expenses of a designated beneficiary (maybe your child). There's two types: a pre-paid plan, and a savings plan. It is a way to put money away for future college expenses. The money you put in is after tax money, but it grows tax free over the years, and when the money is taken out it is not taxed. Not all states allow it, and for those that do, the money you put in could be before state tax is assessed. Look into it when the time comes.

Loans

One of the ways that banks make money is by loaning out the money we have deposited. We often need money to buy a house, property, or a car. These loans are named differently because of the way that the interest you pay is calculated. You can get a loan to go on vacation or do some remodeling of your house, but you need collateral. Collateral means that you have something of value to guarantee that you can pay off the loan. For example, you might have property or some stock to put up as collateral.

Mortgages

When you want to buy a house or property, the loan is called a mortgage. For mortgages, the process of paying it back is called amortization which is essentially a compounding method. A good way to think about a 30 year fixed mortgage is that you don't have one single loan, but rather individual loans with terms of 360 months, then one for 359 months, then one for 358 months and so on, all strung together.

Each month sees a payment calculated with a smaller loan balance over the new shorter term, and while the total of the payment remains the same, the amount of interest you pay in a given month decreases while the amount of principal you pay increases. This is a process known as "amortization."

There are fixed rate mortgages and adjustable or variable rate mortgages, and there are fixed (or adjustable) rate mortgages with a balloon. Fixed rate mortgages are just that... the interest is fixed for the term of the loan. With the adjustable or variable rate mortgage, the interest rate can change within the term of the loan. The mortgage with the balloon sets a time in which the loan must be paid off in full or renegotiated. Try to avoid a balloon type mortgage unless you fully understand the terms.

A good way to take out a mortgage is to take out a 30 year fixed mortgage (to keep the payments low) with the option to prepay. Then, in the future as your salary increases, you pay more than you are supposed to with the extra money going to reduce the principal.

Auto Loans

Auto loans are called installment loans and they can be of two types:
1. Simple interest add-on or
2. Simple interest amortizing

Simple interest add-on loans are actually written as a single loan. The monthly payment is the principal plus the total sum of interest, divided by the number of months. Each payment consists of exactly the same amount of principal and interest, and as such, <u>there's no savings to be had from prepaying these kinds of loans early.</u>

Simple interest loans can be either simple or compound. Simple interest accrues only on the principal, but compound interest accrues on both principal and interest. Accrues means that the interest accumulates or builds. The difference you pay on a $10,000, five year auto loan at 5% could be over $1,500. Keep it simple.

Simple interest amortizing loans work similar to a mortgage with a declining loan balance and declining term producing a constant monthly payment with changing compositions of principal and interest. Prepaying these can save you some money.

A loan to avoid: There can also still be loans based upon a thing called the "Rule of 78." These are simple interest add-on loans with a twist; they are structured to have you pay the interest due on the loan first, then once that's done, your payments will cover the principal.

These should be avoided, since you end up "renting" money during the early years of the loan while your principal doesn't decline. If you should hold the loan to term, there is no difference in total cost when compared to a standard simple interest add-on loan, but if you should need to pay the loan off early, you'll find that you still owe most -- if not all -- of the original loan despite having made payments for some period of time.

The point is that you need to know what the repayment terms are for the loan you are taking out whether it be a mortgage or a car loan. For mortgages you want fixed interest with the option to prepay (without penalty). With car loans, make certain you understand the terms of repayment.

Plastic Money (Credit cards and Debit cards)

Credit cards can be hazardous to your wealth if not very carefully managed. A transaction on a credit card is a loan from the credit card company to you. The interest rate you will pay on your unpaid balance often ranges from 15% to 30% or more per year (after the very low introductory rate). The card companies make it easy to get deep into debt by allowing you to pay a minimum balance every month, but by paying off your balance this way could take years even if you don't put any new charges on your card.

Some people have gotten themselves into very deep financial trouble by maxing out several cards then taking out a bank loan to consolidate to pay off all the cards, then maxing out the cards again and again.

NOTE: If you find yourself deep in debt and seek out a debt counseling service, watch out. Some are actually fronts for the credit card companies. Their only interest is getting you to pay off the cards first.

The best way to use credit cards is to pay the balance in full when you get the statement thereby avoiding paying any interest. You can set up an automatic payment schedule whereby the money is taken automatically from your checking or savings account in part or in full. Credit card companies don't especially like it when you do this, but they make so much money on people who do pay interest, they just consider you a nuisance. (They also make money on what they charge the store.) Some card companies are beginning to assess a monthly service charge when people pay the balance in full each month.

In the event you should accidentally miss a payment, they charge a very hefty penalty charge and may raise your interest rate forever, and affect your credit rating.

Unless you have just come back from the moon, you've seen the ads that say that certain cards pay you back for using their card. Credit card conditions have more "gotchas" than you can shake a stick at. You've seen that some give you points for air fare while some others give you a percentage for what you spend on gas, restaurants, clothes, etc.. You've got to check the fine print because they may pay only if you only go to certain gas stations or certain restaurants.

One card that I have from a membership warehouse sends me a check every year, but I must continue to be a member and must go to the store to cash it. Gotcha!

One other thing with credit cards… watch the very fine print unless you want to be hit with an annual charge or a greater interest rate after the first 'introductory' year.

Debit card transactions take the money directly out of your checking account. These are not loans. With debit cards you can make cash withdrawals when you make a purchase saving ATM fees. There can be different liability issues if your card or I.D. is stolen. Check with your bank.

NEVER, NEVER EVER GIVE SOMEONE YOUR USER NAME, PINS AND PASSWORDS!

Account Security While considering security, you should change your User Names, PINS, and Passwords often if you use online banking. You should also check with the three major credit bureaus (Experian, Equifax, and TransUnion).

By law, you are entitled to one FREE credit report from one of the three bureaus. The only truly free annual credit report comes from *annualcreditreport.com*. So, each year, get your free report from one of the bureaus. You can set up a plan where no one can open an account, apply for a loan, or take out a credit card in your name without verification from you.

You should also check your account activity more often than once a month. If your personal ID has been stolen, the thief might first make a small charge to your account to see if you are watching. Then, if it is not caught, he can clean you out.

If your bank or credit union offers security features, take advantage of them. One that I especially like is that the bank must verify with you if a transaction exceeds a monetary limit that you establish. It could be a nuisance, but well worth it.

Just a last minute thought… anytime that I travel outside of my home area, I contact my card companies to inform that I am going away. This can prevent embarrassment if the security section of your card company stops service because the transaction occurred outside of your usual home area.

The quality, not the longevity, of one's life is what is important.
—Dr. Martin Luther King

Chapter 3
Insurance
Life, Auto & Health

Here's some basic information that applies to almost every type of insurance:

- Group policies are usually cheaper than private policies.
- Your agent is not always the best one to give you good advice because he is torn between giving you the advice that is best for you and making a hefty commission. (Besides commissions there are also bonuses and rewards for writing so many policies a year.)
- Get a policy with the highest deductible you can afford. Deductible means that before the company pays you, you have to pay something first. For example, if you had a claim for $100, and you have a $30 deductible, you'd have to pay the $30 before the company would pay their $70. If you had chosen a $10 deductible policy, the company would pay $90, but your premium for the policy would be greater.
- Insurance companies are in the business of making money... not paying benefits.
- Insurance companies can often use common words, but attach different meanings than we do. Usually their language works to their benefit not yours.
- Purchase policies from strong companies not fly-by-nighters.
- Read the fine print. Get written explanations when you're confused. Lean toward policies written in common English not insurance babble.
- Agents tend to want to attach all kinds of extras for the purpose of padding their commission. These extras may cost just pennies a day, but they are expensive and unnecessary.

LIFE INSURANCE

Everyone needs life insurance, but how much and what kind? There are two types of life insurance policies: term and whole life (also called cash value, universal, variable, or permanent). Term life insurance is just plain insurance on your life to pay the limits of the policy if you should die during the term of the policy.

Whole life (and its many hybrids) is much more complicated and is composed of two different financial products: life insurance coupled with an investment.

The premium for whole life can be as much as ten times that of term life for the same amount of coverage and the commission for the selling agent can be over 100% of the first year's premium. Think of whole life this way… every time you go out to buy a loaf of bread, you pay an extra twenty-five cents to the bakery which they invest and give back to you years later along with some interest. So, I ask you, do you want bread or bread with some savings that you might get years and years in the future? With term insurance there are no savings plan, no tax benefits, no retirement plan, and no borrowing. Regardless which policy you buy, be certain that the policy is guaranteed renewable.

Consumer Reports has, for many years, recommended term life insurance as the simplest, least expensive option which allows you to get the maximum coverage for the least cost.

Group policies can often be cheaper than private policies, but you risk losing your coverage when you lose your job or develop a medical condition that could render you uninsurable. (This may change with Obamacare.)

Only you can decide how much coverage you need. A term policy for a forty year old man, in good health, can go for $660 whereas the same whole life policy could cost $6,760 a year. Rates vary from company to company So, do you need coverage or do you need an investment?

How much life insurance coverage do you need? A fee-only financial planner in San Diego recommends at least one million for a family with a stay-at-home mother. Every family is different, but when you sit down to think about it, the total can get large. You can use an online calculator available at *360financialliteracy.org*.

You can shop for the lowest rates for term life insurance at a number of online sites such as:
Accuquote.com,
Selectquote.com, and
Findmyinsurance.com.

For whole life insurance rates, go to: *Lifeinsurance.com*

The best way to get a comprehensive plan for insurance and investment is to find a "fee only" financial advisor and/or insurance consultant. Insurance agents get paid for what they sell, whereas "fee only" advisors get paid a flat fee. The Consumer Federation of America can also help you to compare policies (for a fee) at *evaluatelifeinsurance.org*. For a fee only financial consultant, go to cfp.net or for a fee-only financial advisors go to napfa.org.

I also suggest using a broker instead of an agent. Agents usually sell for one company whereas an insurance broker sells for many different companies and can do the searching for the best rates for you.

Now, if you thought life insurance was a mess, wait until you get into auto insurance.

AUTO INSURANCE
Auto insurance involves many different types of coverage:

Collision insurance pays for the repair or replacement of the <u>policy owner's</u> car in the event of an accident regardless who caused the accident.

Collision coverage usually requires the payment of a deductible when a claim is made and may be required to secure a new car loan.

Comprehensive insurance is an often misunderstood term. People think of it as "all encompassing", but in auto insurance terms, it has a different meaning. Comprehensive coverage protects the policy owner against damages to the car that are the result of covered perils not related to a collision such as:

- Theft
- Vandalism
- Fire
- Natural disasters like a hurricane or a tornado
- Falling objects
- Damage done to your car by animals
- A civil disturbance

A common question is: Should I buy comprehensive and collision coverage if I have an older car?

The answer is – **it depends**.

Since the comprehensive and collision coverage benefit is usually limited to the cash value of your vehicle, one way to lower auto insurance premiums is to raise the deductible and/or to drop the comprehensive and collision coverage on an older car. Why carry comprehensive coverage with a low deductible if you are not concerned about minor cosmetic damage to your vehicle? If your vehicle is not looking brand new, is paid for, and may be providing its last few good miles, then not buying comprehensive coverage might be a good way to save some money on your insurance.

Remember – if you drop comprehensive (or collision) coverage, you are responsible for the full cost of repairs or replacement. So balance the option of lower car insurance premiums with your ability to pay out-of-pocket for uncovered expenses.

Experts suggest that if your annual premium for collision and comprehensive coverage equals or exceeds 10% of the cash value of your vehicle, you could consider dropping it.

Bodily injury liability pays (up to your policy limits) for injuries or death for which you or other drivers, covered by your car insurance policy, are found to be responsible for in a motor vehicle accident. Policy terms vary but typically bodily injury liability insurance will pay, up to your policy limits, for:

- Medical expenses
- Funeral expenses
- Loss of income
- Pain and suffering
- Legal defense if a lawsuit results from the auto accident

Policy limits for bodily injury liability are per person and per accident and coverage is written as such. For example, $25,000/$50,000 means that the maximum payout per person is $25,000, and the maximum payout for all people injured in one accident is $50,000. This coverage may also be simply written as 25/50.

Bodily injury liability does NOT cover your injuries, <u>only the injuries of others for which you are judged to be liable for.</u> For your personal injuries to be covered, you would need personal injury protection (PIP).

Uninsured (and underinsured) motorist insurance pays for medical bills, and those of your passengers, if you are hit by a driver who is uninsured or underinsured. It may also cover pain and suffering and lost income. In cases where the other driver has insurance, but isn't enough to cover the bills, underinsured motorist bodily injury makes up the difference between his policy limits and yours.

Uninsured motorist property damage will pay your deductible in some states if you also carry collision coverage; otherwise, it will pay a predetermined amount, usually around $3,500, toward your repairs. Underinsured motorist property damage does the same when the other driver's policy is insufficient. Different states have different laws.

Accidental death benefit pays if, in a covered auto accident, bodily injury causes the death of you or a covered family member. The benefit paid is according to the terms of your specific policy.

Roadside assistance coverage may pay for towing (for a certain number of miles), lost keys, getting your car started, etc.. Many drivers are members of AAA or other organizations that have better coverage.

There are many considerations when taking out auto insurance: What kind of coverage, how much coverage, and what deductible? The lower the deductible, the higher the premium. You can cut your premium by as much as 9% by changing the deductible from $500 to $1,000, but if you have an accident, can you afford to pay out the $1,000? Your decision.

NOTE: If, for various reasons you opt out of collision and comprehensive coverage, you might have to purchase insurance from a rental company when you rent a car. However, some credit card companies include this coverage when you use their card to rent a car. You might also NOT be covered if you happen to borrow someone else's vehicle. CHECK WITH YOUR INSURANCE and CREDIT CARD COMPANIES!

HEALTH INSURANCE

The whole issue of health insurance is complicated and confusing especially since enactment of the Affordable Care Act (Obamacare). One thing is absolutely certain, you and your family need it. Here's some basic information:

HMO (Health Maintenance Organization) If you are enrolled in an HMO you will receive most or all of your health care from a network provider. HMO's require that you select a primary care physician (PCP) who is responsible for managing and coordinating all of your health care needs.

Your PCP (often called a gatekeeper) will serve as your personal doctor to provide all of your basic healthcare services. PCPs include internal medicine physicians, family physicians, and in some HMOs, gynecologists who provide basic healthcare for women. For your children, you can select a pediatrician or a family physician to be their PCP.

If you need care from a physician specialist in the network or a diagnostic service such as a lab test or x-ray, your primary care physician (PCP) will have to provide you with a referral. If you do not have a referral or you choose to go to a doctor outside of your HMO's network, you will most likely have to pay all or most of the cost for that care.

In addition to monthly premiums, you will have deductibles and co-pay guidelines. A co-pay is different than a deductible. A deductible, as mentioned before, is something you have to pay before the insurance company pays their portion. A co-pay is something you pay up front to get service. For example, when you go to see the doctor, you must pay $10 before you can see the doctor.

PPO A Preferred Provider Organization is a health plan that has contracts with a network of "preferred" providers from which you can choose. You do not need to select a PCP and you may or may not need referrals to see other providers in the network.

If you receive your care from a doctor in the preferred network, you will only be responsible for your annual deductible (a feature of some PPOs) and a copayment for your visit. If you get health services from a doctor or hospital that is not in the preferred network (known as going "out-of-network") you will pay a higher amount, and you will need to pay the doctor directly and then file a claim with the PPO to get reimbursed.

How do HMOs and PPOs differ?

Which health care providers must I choose?
HMO: You must choose doctors, hospitals, and other providers in the HMO network.

PPO: You can choose doctors, hospitals, and other providers from the PPO network or from out-of-network. If you choose an out-of-network provider, you most likely will pay more.

Do I need to have a primary care physician (PCP)?
HMO: Yes, your HMO will not provide coverage if you do not have a PCP.

PPO: No, you can receive care from any doctor you choose. But remember, you will pay more if the doctors you choose are not "preferred" providers.

How do I get to see a specialist?

HMO: You will need a referral from your PCP to see a specialist (such as a cardiologist or surgeon) except in emergency situations. Your PCP also must refer you to a specialist who is in the HMO network.

PPO: You do not need a referral to see a specialist. However, some specialists will only see patients who are referred to them by a primary care doctor. And, some PPOs require that you get a prior approval for certain expensive services, such as MRIs.

Do I have to file any insurance claims?

HMO: All of the providers in the HMO network are required to file a claim to get paid. You do not have to file a claim, and your provider may not charge you directly or send you a bill.

PPO: If you get your healthcare from a network provider you usually do not need to file a claim. However, if you go out of network for services you may have to pay the provider in full and then file a claim with the PPO to get reimbursed. The money you receive from the PPO will most likely be only part of the bill. You are responsible for any part of the doctor's fee that the PPO does not pay.

How do I pay for services in the network?

HMO: The only charges you should incur for in-network services are copayments for doctor's visits and other services such as procedures and prescriptions.

PPO: In most PPO networks you will only be responsible for the copayment. Some PPOs do have an annual deductible for any services, in network or out of network.

How do I pay for services out of the network?

HMO: Except for certain types of care that may not be available from a network provider, you are not covered for any out-of-network services.

PPO: If you choose to go outside the PPO network for your care, you will need to pay the provider and then get reimbursed by the PPO. Most likely, you will have to pay an annual deductible and coinsurance. For example, if the out-of-network doctor charged you $200 for a visit, you are responsible for the full amount if you have not met your deductible. If you have met the deductible, the PPO may pay 60%, or $120 and you will pay 40%, or $80.

Most people have to take the insurance plan provided by their employer, but if you are purchasing health insurance on your own, here's a couple of mistakes you can make:

1. Not getting health insurance because you are healthy. Bad idea.
2. Picking a health plan only because the premiums are the lowest.
3. Going out of network… can cost you a bundle.
4. Not taking advantage of flexible spending accounts which let you set aside tax free money from your paycheck to pay for medical expenses not covered by insurance such as deductibles and co-payments.

Insurance Policies You Don't Need
You can get insurance for just about anything imaginable. I read somewhere that you can get a policy protecting you in the event you are abducted by aliens. More down to earth though, I Googled for "insurance policies you don't need" and found several sources. Here's a list most agreed upon:

1. Credit card insurance
2. Dread disease insurance
3. Cell phone insurance
4. ID theft insurance
5. Flight insurance
6. Mortgage insurance (May depend on the amount of   deposit you have.)
7. Extended warranty insurance
8 Rental car insurance
9 Water line (utility) insurance
10 Flood (Unless you live in a flood prone area of course.)
11 Accidental death insurance
12 Automobile collision insurance (May be required by   your finance company.)

If you Google as I did, you will get good explanations as to why these policies are unnecessary… plus others.

*It's not the events in your life that change you,
it is your reaction to those events.*
Many authors – Several translations

Chapter 4
How to Purchase a Vehicle

In many foreign countries, bargaining is a way of life. There's a skill involved, and people become accustomed to it. But here in the USA, nothing matches the way we go about buying a car or truck. Generally speaking, Americans do not like to bargain... and dealers know it. Not only do we not like to negotiate a price, but often there's emotion involved in the process and we have no idea what is a fair price. All we know is that we want to pay less than the sticker price.

Nowadays we have many more ways of buying a vehicle than in years past. AAA, Costco, and many other companies can negotiate a price for you. Some vehicle companies advertise that they have a no-haggle policy... that their prices are already rock bottom. But, how can you know that you are getting a good deal unless you've done a lot of shopping and research on your own?

New or used auto/truck dealers have bad reputations. They are experts at what they do. You are an innocent victim of a highly trained and orchestrated effort to separate you from as much money as possible. Between the price of the vehicle you intend to buy, what they want to give you for a trade-in, any extras they can get you to agree to buy, and financing arrangements... you are going to lose a lot more money than you intend to lose.

Before you get caught, go online, to the library, or book store and find yourself a good book on the subject. Every year, *Consumer Reports* magazine carries excellent articles on car/truck buying. A good book to look for is *How to Outwit any Auto, Truck, or RV Dealer Every Time* by JD Gallant. Also, check out *edmunds.com* and *kbb.com*

Another thing, be sure to get a Carfax report. You know all the vehicles that get caught in floods, tornados, etc.? They have been known to show up on new and used car lots. If the dealer doesn't get one for you, get your own. Same if you are buying from a private party.

Dealers are full of tricks to get you to buy and to separate you from your hard earned money. For example, dealers have been known to bug the part of the showroom where you are sitting so that they can overhear your private conversations with your car buying companion while the salesperson is away checking on something.

At one dealership I let the mechanic take my car so that he could give me a price on my trade-in. Meanwhile, the salesperson worked his charm on me. After a reasonable time, wanting to leave, I requested that my keys be returned to me, but they always had an excuse to keep me there a little longer. Finally, I grabbed the phone and started calling 911. I got my keys real fast.

One other time I had done all my research. I knew which brand, make, and model along with what options I wanted. I had visited several showrooms and I knew what prices they were asking. I had read my books and magazines and I knew what price I should pay for the vehicle I wanted. A dealership several miles away had placed an ad in the Sunday newspaper advertising exactly the car I wanted at the price I was willing to pay. So, I called my local dealer and told him exactly what I wanted and the price I wanted to pay. I told him that if he could find the car I wanted and was willing to take the price I was offering, then call me back and we'd have a deal.

A couple of hours later he called to say that we had a deal. Excitedly, my wife and I went to the dealership, but instead of the car I'd asked for, they'd put out a beautiful, bright red convertible. They swore that this was a better model with more options which I knew was not true because I had done my research. Oh yes, it was the same price.

Angrily we started to walk away, with the salesperson following close behind. He then admitted that they did have what I'd asked for, but it had options that I had not requested and they would cost $500.00 more.

We continued to walk. Several steps later he relented and agreed to remove most of the options we didn't want, but we'd have to pay for the options he could not remove. We continued to walk. By the time I put the key in my car door, he agreed to sell me the car I wanted including the extra options without extra cost. Deal!

We went back to his little cubicle and he put together the sales agreement. As I took the pen to sign, I noticed that an additional $100 had been added to the sales agreement as a miscellaneous expense. My wife and I got up and started to walk out again. The salesperson said, "I can't believe that you're letting a meager $100 stand in the way of this fantastic agreement." I replied, "And I can't believe you'd let me walk out for a meager $100." He promptly scratched out the $100 entry and we finally signed the papers.

When buying a new or used vehicle, from a dealer or a private party, there are four ingredients that you MUST keep in mind:
1. The price of the vehicle.
2. The value of your trade in… if you have one.
3. Financing
4. Options

Dealers like to package the first three together. By doing so, they are able to confuse the buyer and make more money on the transaction. To be successful, you, the buyer, should treat them all separately.

BUYING A USED CAR

Getting to the price of the vehicle

Most people, if given the choice, would prefer to buy a brand new car with all of its new features and gadgets, but if for financial reasons you look into a used car, take heart. There can be advantages to buying a used one.

First, you won't take that immediate depreciation loss when you drive a new car off the lot. A car, just a couple of years old will not depreciate as steeply. Some financial advisors suggest that you should never buy a new car, but should look for good vehicles about two years old.

Secondly, taxes and insurance costs are lower for the used car. On the other hand, financing costs may be a little higher. Many people sell their new cars after having them only three years even though they may not be having any trouble with them. These can make especially good buys. The median age of cars on the road in year 2000 was 8.3 years vs. 5.9 years in 1979. So, used cars don't have to carry the risk they used to carry. A car that's been well cared for can last well over the 200,000 mile mark. However, to be sure to get the value you are expecting, follow some basic steps. (Check out *Consumer Reports* Used Car issue and KBB.)

When you start hitting the car lots, bring along paper, pencil, and calculator. If you happen to have a copy of *Consumer Reports* or a book on buying a vehicle, carry it with you too.

Step 1   Do some research

For a nominal fee, *Consumer Reports* Used Car Service will get you financial and reliability information for the car you are looking at (1-800-258-1169). You need to find out the retail price and the trade in price. These are the top and bottom numbers from which you begin to negotiate. Mileage, condition of the vehicle, and extras may add or detract from these numbers. The *Consumer Reports* will also send you information on the reliability of the vehicle in question.

The *Kelly Blue Book*, the bible of car value, will also give you the financial information as will the N.A.S.D. book. Both can be found at a library, bookstore, or local bank. *Kbb.com*

Step 2   Negotiate the price

Armed with the information you gathered, you can now begin to negotiate a price. The final price you decide to pay should be somewhere between the book value and the dealer's price. Your first offer should be closer to the lower number. Any future counter offers you make should be in small increments up from your first offer, not down from the sellers top price. After your final offer has been turned down and you are still not happy, give the seller your name and number and tell him to call you when he changes his mind. At all times keep the negotiations casual and friendly.

Step 3 Inspection

President Ronald Reagan used to say of the Russians, "Trust, but verify." When you and the seller have come to an agreement on the final price, make arrangements to have the car inspected by an independent mechanic before signing any paperwork or handing over any money. It will cost you a few dollars, but it can save you a bundle later on. Of course, using the *Consumer Reports* service for their reliability ratings will help a lot too, but don't just go by the report.

At the time of settlement, make sure the VIN number is the same on the car as on the documents. Also make certain you have a clear title and a bill of sale for the vehicle. Check out carfax.com

Step 4 Final Precautions

When purchasing a used car from a dealership, you might be encouraged to purchase insurance that will pay for any unexpected breakdowns within the first few years. Generally these are not such a good idea. The insurance company knows, in great detail, what the chances are that certain things will break down. The premium is intended to cover those possibilities and show a profit besides. You can also purchase an extended warranty policy aside from the dealership for less.

When buying from a dealer, make certain you clearly understand the conditions of any warranty that might come with the car. Make certain that anything the dealer promises to do is clearly written on the bill of sale. Verbal agreements stand for nothing.

Finally, if your bill of sale says, "AS IS" then you have absolutely no recourse once you take possession of the vehicle. Try to get a dealer warranty for at least a few months.

BUYING A NEW CAR

Buying a new car is a little different than buying a used car, but you still must do your research. One of the best places again is the *Consumer Reports* magazine and their research resources. They can give you the price the dealer paid for the vehicle which is the starting point for any negotiation allowing for a 3-5% mark-up by the dealer. Their report will also give you info on rebates and incentives. To get their report, call 1-800-657-7378 and ask for their New Car Price Service.

Dealers will also try to sell you extras like undercoating, rust proofing, fabric protection, payment protection, extended warranties, etc. which are generally not recommended. But watch out...this salesperson is an expert. These services are very high profit items and the salesperson works on commission.

When negotiating the price of the new car, do not include your trade-in or financing into the negotiation. Keep all three separate. They won't like it so be prepared to be firm.

The Trade-In

The amount you can reasonably expect to get for your trade-in can be determined similar to the way you decided on the price you were willing to pay for the used car. By first finding the top and bottom figures for your make, model, age, and condition, you will have a price range from which to begin negotiating.

Depending on your personal situation, you can usually get more for your old car, and get a better price for the new car you are buying, if you sell your old car yourself rather than trading it in at the dealer.

Whether selling your old car through the dealer or to a private party, you can expect to get a better deal if the vehicle is clean inside and out, body work is done to cover dents, scratches, and rust, and you have maintenance records and receipts available.

Financing

Almost from the first minute you walk onto the lot, the salesperson will try to learn how you plan to finance your car. He might be up front and ask directly, but more often than not, he will ask innocent questions to keep you off your guard, but will be able to learn your financing plans from your answers. The dealership will push, in very subtle ways, to finance your purchase because they may get a kick-back from the bank or they might have their own finance company..

Before you start to look around, check out more than one source of financing for rates. Not all rates are the same or calculated the same.

Find out exactly what each $100 will cost you for a given loan period. Try to get pre-approved by the lending institution. (Credit unions might have a better rate than a bank.) If you are turned down, try to find out why and how you can get around it. If the dealership learns that you must finance through them, you are dead meat. Try to avoid dealer financing if at all possible. Dealer financing is not a convenience to you. It's a cash cow for the dealer. Do not let the salesperson tie financing with the sales price of the car or the trade-in. Keep them all separate.

If you do talk about dealer financing you must get four figures:
1.   The total amount to be financed.
2.   The interest rate.
3.   The term (length of time you will be making payments).
4.   Your monthly payment.

Before signing anything, check the figures carefully!!! Compare the payment quoted against what you learned when you called the bank earlier.

Between the cost of cars being so expensive and lasting longer, five years should be the maximum term of your car loan. So many car buyers have had to ditch their cars before it's paid off leaving them in a financial hole before they purchase a replacement. Consider this: If you can't pay it off in five years, perhaps you can't afford it…. and should wait.

If you keep your car after the loan is paid off it's a good idea to continue putting some money away each month in a separate account as though you are still paying on the loan. The advantages are:
1.   You will prevent wasting the money.
2.   You will have money set aside for needed repairs on your old car.
3.   You will have money set aside for a nice down payment on your next car which will help offset the higher price of the new car due to inflation.

When trying to decide on a new car or a used car, keep in mind that the interest rate for a used car is higher than the interest rate of a new car. It might be possible, when considering financing and the price of the car, to wind up paying more for a used car than a new one. Keep your calculator handy and don't make a decision on the spot. Take time to work the numbers. All that math you had in school might begin to pay off.

Summary:
1. The salesperson is not your bosom buddy. Keep your situation to yourself. Any information you give out can be a weapon used against you.
2. Keep all three elements of the deal separate: the price of the vehicle, the trade-in price, and financing.
3. Do your research.
4. Get pre-approved financing.
5. Check everything before signing right up to the very last minute… on everything.
6. Bring paper, pencil, calculator, magazines, and books with you.
7. Bring along someone who knows the ropes. I prefer not to bring my wife until I'm serious about buying. This always gives me the excuse, "I'll have to go back and get my wife before signing."
8. Beware of what's called the Back End Expert. Here you will be encouraged to purchase unneeded services such as undercoating, fabric protection, extended warranties, VIN etching, paint sealant, wheel-nut locks, etc.. All not worth the price, or necessary.

LEASING A CAR

There are not many good reasons and lots of bad reasons to lease a car. Oh, I know it sounds good, but watch out. Leasing can be more complicated than buying, and more complicated can only mean more gotcha's. Remember, that I said that there were four things to buying a car? Well, there's lots more than four when you lease. Enough said.

Resources:
1. www.carsdirect.com & www.carorder.com are direct order web sites
2. www.edmunds.com is an encyclopedia of all kinds of car facts
3. www.leasesource.com provides leasing information

4. www.nhtsa.dot.gov & www.highwaysafety.org give you safety information
5. www.kbb.com is the *Kelly Blue Book* site or call 800-258-3266
6. www.intellichoice.com give you a lot of cost information on recent and old models
7. www.dealernet.com connects you to thousands of dealers nationwide
8. www.autotrader.com is a place to find used cars for sale
9. *Consumer Reports* magazine and web site

If nothing ever changed, there'd be no butterflies.
— *Author Unknown*

Chapter 5
Investing

This chapter might be a little premature since most of you probably don't have enough money to invest. However, it is NEVER too early to start putting money aside. No matter how little you earn, your expenses will always be just a little bit more, so if you can set a certain amount aside, before you see it, your spending will adjust. You should have short term and long term savings plans.

There are many, many ways to save money without real sacrifice. For example, when you go to a restaurant, do you ask for coffee or a soft drink? Water is free! How about those fancy drinks at coffee shops? Do you need designer clothes? Every little bit helps.

The first thing to consider is how to get the most from what little money you have. Your bank will have savings accounts, but by going online you can find banks or credit unions that have better rates of interest. MMA's and MMF's generally pay better rates than passbook savings. CD's usually pay even more, but your money will be tied up for a pre-determined period of time. Once you get a little nest egg put aside, you can start thinking about real investing in stocks and bonds.

I don't want to get into any real detail here, but for your information, here's a few definitions:

Stocks   A share of stock is a fractional share of ownership in a business. There are two main types of stock: common and preferred. Common stock usually entitles the owner to vote at shareholders' meetings and to receive dividends. Preferred stock generally does not have voting rights, but has a higher claim on assets and earnings than the common shares. Owners of preferred stock receive dividends before common shareholders and have priority in the event that a company goes bankrupt and is liquidated.

You can buy one share, but it is usually best to buy in lots of 100 shares. Less than 100 shares is called an "odd lot".

Mutual Funds A mutual fund pools money together from thousands of small investors and then its manager buys stocks, bonds or other securities with it. When you buy a share of a mutual fund, you get a stake in all its investments. Since most funds allow you to begin investing with as little as a thousand dollars, you can attain a diversified portfolio for much less than you could buying individual stocks and bonds. Plus, you don't have to worry about keeping track of dozens of holdings - that's the fund manager's job. Mutual funds offer great diversification.

You can purchase a mutual fund made up of shares of stock from only steel companies, or only healthcare companies. Vanguard, a popular investment company, has a mutual fund called "Total Stock Market Index Fund". This fund is composed of hundreds of different companies.

There are "loaded" and "non-loaded" mutual funds. The term "load" refers to a fee to purchase. There are front loaded and back loaded funds where you either pay a fee to buy or a fee to sell. No-load funds have no fee.

Bonds A bond is an 'IOU' in which an investor agrees to loan money to a company or government in exchange for a predetermined interest rate for a pre-determined length of time. If a business wants to expand, one of its options is to borrow money from individual investors, pension funds, or mutual funds. The company issues bonds at various interest rates and sells them to the public. Investors purchase them with the understanding that the company will pay back their original principal (the amount the investor loaned to the company) by a specific date (this is called the "maturity" date). Meanwhile, you get to enjoy the interest income.

Who can issue bonds? Governments, (states, municipalities, cities, etc.), a variety of institutions, and corporations. Bonds should be held for long periods of time, not bought and sold quickly like stocks. A CD is similar to a bond.

The interest received from corporate bonds is taxable whereas municipal bonds may not be taxable. This fact can be important depending upon your income tax bracket.

You will see a lot about short, intermediate, and long term bonds. This refers to the length of time before maturity, and each term offers a different interest rate and volatility (how quickly its value changes due to interest rates).

You can invest in bond funds which can be a mix of terms and different companies. Some people will buy bonds from one company, but "ladder" the terms the same as they would do with CD's.

IMPORTANT: the value of a bond changes inversely to interest rates. That means that the value of a bond goes down as interest rates go up. So, if you are in a bond fund, keep track of interest rate trends.

When purchasing corporate or government bonds, you must understand the rating system which refers to their credit worthiness published by credit rating agencies. Moody's, Standard and Poor, and Fitch are prominent rating services. Ratings can be reported as high as AAA to as low as D.

If the issuer of the bond goes bankrupt, you will probably lose your money. Ever hear of junk bonds? That's what they are… junk.

Annuities are more associated with insurance companies than with investment companies. They come in different flavors, and are highly, highly complex. They are known to have very high commissions. Therefore, they are aggressively marketed.

Unless you can understand what the agent is telling you, stay away. And, even if you think you do, check it out.

Life is the sum of your choices.
— Albert Camus

Chapter 6
Getting and Keeping a Job

This chapter about being an employee is aimed more at the college graduate or experienced/skilled person looking for a job or the beginning of a career, rather than the teenager looking for a job at the local burger joint. However, there are many points of commonality.

From the employer's point of view...

Employers often find that young employees have a hard time making the transition from doing work at home for free to working for someone else for a salary. Some, unfortunately, never seem to make the adjustment. They go from job to job their whole life often blaming other people for their inability to hold a job for any length of time. If you thought that your parents were demanding, an employer is often much, much more demanding at the work place. The standards that used to be acceptable at home just won't cut it on the job.

Several years ago, a friend of mine was invited to participate in a high school career day event. Being a dentist, he spoke to students who were interested in becoming dental assistants. After his presentation, one of the students made the comment that it seemed that every time she went to her dentist's office, there were different people working for him. Her concern was that the job did not seem to have any job security.

He asked her, "What does your bedroom look like?"

She turned a couple of shades of red and the rest of the class started to giggle in equal embarrassment.

The point he was trying to make was that after treating a patient, he would ask the assistant to prepare the room for the next patient.

Unfortunately, some assistants cleaned the treatment room as though it was their bedroom at home.

Let me be frank with you… as an employer, I have too much to teach you without having to go and teach you what you should have learned on your mother's knee. I don't have the time, or the inclination. I expect you to be able to speak appropriately, act appropriately, and dress appropriately. The success of my business, for which I have worked many years, the business into which I have invested a lot of money, the livelihood of my other employees, my livelihood, and the welfare of my family… all depend upon you, and I don't care if you are a ditch digger or a hospital physician. OK, I got that off my chest.

Another problem is that we often spend years and years studying to accumulate knowledge and skills to get a job, yet never learn <u>how</u> to be an employee. In my experience as both an employer and an employee, I've seen many people quit or be fired because they lacked employee skills, not job skills.

What does it cost an employer to have an employee? The fact is, it costs an employer much more than you'd expect. First, regardless of your salary, the employer spends at least 23% more for your Social Security, Workman's Comp., and Unemployment Insurance. So, if you are making $400 a week, it is costing him, right off the top, another $93. Now, add to that the cost to him for your health plan, sick days, vacation days, and paid holidays… and that does not include a retirement plan and/or child care benefits. This also doesn't include the cost of advertising, interviewing, and training the new employee. Considering all of the above, you can see why business is reluctant to hire new employees unless they can justify the expense.

So, between the application you fill out, the resume, and the interview… the employer is looking for the person who can best fit the needs of his business. <u>For the most part, employers are looking for people with good basic knowledge in their chosen field, but who are also honest, dependable, and who show up on time.</u> Oh yes, and can think. It's that simple.

From the employee's point of view:

When an employer puts a sign in the window or places an ad in the paper advertising an open position, the employer in effect begins a process of shopping that is similar to the process you use when shopping at the mall. The employer is looking for the best value, the best deal possible for the money to be spent.

You, the employee need to find work to earn money to get on with your life. You might even have a family to support. One problem you have is that you have hundreds, maybe thousands of people looking for the same job. After all, you all graduated from high school or college at the same time. How do you stand out so that you get the job?

To do this you must understand what the employer needs. What's the job description and, what are the goals of the company? Boiled down to its essence, the employer wants someone who will help him to make money, increase his business, and improve profits. That's the bottom line... to make money, increase business, and improve profits. Your job is to convince the employer that you can fulfill those goals better than anyone else.

A friend of mine once advertised for an office secretary. Over 80 young ladies applied for the position. All were recent graduates of the local high school, business, or secretarial school. After going through all of the interviews, reading all the resumes, and reviewing his interview notes, he had narrowed it down to about 20 identical candidates. He had to make a decision. Whom did he hire? He chose a young lady with an unusual nickname. The point of the story is that putting job qualifications aside, there are many, many other factors that influence the hiring decision.

Most employers will first sort through the many applications they get and boil them down to the most promising candidates. Believe me, this is not hard to do. What do you think an employer would do if he saw on an application with misspellings, poor grammar, scratching out, or profanity all on lined paper? Then he picks another one up that is nicely written on nice stationary without errors. Which would you set aside for the personal interview?

Now, here I know I'm going to offend someone and perhaps violate some kind of discrimination laws, but listen to me. A candidate comes in with his pants down around his genitals, he's got tattoos all over his body and multiple piercings. Then, he's got hair all over the place with a blue Mohawk, and his opening line is, "Hey Dude." Now, I fully realize that anyone has the right to look any way they want to look, but on the other hand, the employer should have a right to hire whom he wishes to hire. Yes, I know, I offended someone. The same goes for girls too. Jus sayin.

Before the interview, try to learn, or at least imagine, what you can do to enhance the job you are applying for, keeping in mind the job description and the company's goals. For example, if the job is to answer the phone and take orders, you can say that you can speak clearly; you've been told that your personality comes over the phone; and you are accurate and you pay attention to details. Can you think of any others? Here's a few more:

- Transportation is not a problem because:
  a. I live close by.
  b. I have my own car.
  c. I have a dependable ride.
- I can be at work on time and can give you an eight hour work day.
- This will be my primary job. If I were to find something else to do, this would still be my primary responsibility.
- My penmanship is good. Anyone can read my writing. (Offer a sample)
- I can take orders quickly and accurately.
- I am flexible. I can work days, evenings, and/or weekends. (Employers love flexibility.)
- I can speak and understand another language.
- If you have any kind of work experience that backs up any of your claims, this would be a good time to introduce them. Such as: At my last job, I had a perfect attendance record, at my last job, I used the phone extensively and took orders, or at one of my jobs, we had many Hispanic callers.

The job interview is a two way street. Not only is the employer feeling you out, you have the right to feel him out as well. After all, employment is really a contract. You and the employer have entered into an agreement… a contract. The employer, for a certain sum of money, is hiring you to do a job and provide services for so many hours a day and so many days out of the week. You, on the other hand, have agreed to make yourself available to do the job and provide the services agreed upon. Anything short of this, by either you or the employer, can be considered as theft or at least breach of contract. How would you like to buy a dozen doughnuts and find only 11 in the bag when you get home? The first time might be just an accident, but how many times would it happen before you stopped going to this doughnut shop? On the other hand, would you like to be the doughnut shop owner who got paid with counterfeit money?

Granted, you need a job. You need money, but there are many other things to consider. I had a friend who gave up a job in Pittsburgh, PA for a job near Washington, DC. The reason he made the move was that the new job had a higher salary. The unfortunate thing was that the cost of living in the Washington area was much higher than Pittsburgh's. In the end, he actually had less money in his pocket at the end of the month.

Here are just a few things to think about:
- Will you have a long or short commute?
- Will you have parking fees?
- Who provides and launders the work clothes?
- What's the dress code?
- Are you expected to use your vehicle in the performance of your duties?
- Are you required to join a union?
- Do you have mandatory or voluntary over-time?
- Is there opportunity to work from home once in a while?
- Must you work on holidays with compensatory time off?
- Is day care available either at the work place or nearby?
- How does the cost of living compare to your home area?
- How do you get paid… monthly, weekly, or every two weeks? It makes a difference when the employer pays weekly, every two weeks, or monthly. Don't forget… a month is not 4 weeks. It's closer to 4½ weeks. Take for

example two similar jobs. Job A pays $500 a week while job
B pays $2,000 a month. Which job do you take? Take job
A. Do the math.

Although salary is important considering the points made above, there
are so many other factors to consider. Here's a graph to make my point.

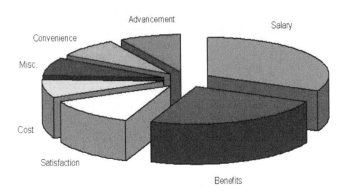

Total Employment Remuneration

Benefits This is usually the second largest consideration and extremely
important. Most people do not realize the value of their benefit
package. Included can be medical insurance, a retirement program,
disability insurance, life insurance, and possibly even a child care
allowance to name a few. Sometimes, in large companies, the employer
allows a certain amount of money to be set aside for benefits and
allows the employee to pick where he/she wants the benefit money
divided.

Suppose you have a working wife who has an excellent medical
package. There's no need for you to use up your benefit money for
another medical package especially if it's inferior. In this case, you
might elect to put your benefit money into a retirement plan. Benefits
may include:

Medical Insurance This is another important and expensive
benefit an employer can offer. Do not underestimate the value of this
benefit. The employer, by covering many employees, can often get a
group rate much cheaper than you can get for yourself. There's no

joking about it… a good medical plan can be very, very expensive. Depending on the size of the company, medical benefits may not be available. You can stay on your parent's insurance until age 26. If you can't, you need to look into getting insurance through the Affordable Care Act.

Retirement Plan This is another big benefit, but often does not appeal to the younger employee. There are several different kinds of plans available. The point of it is that your employer puts a certain percent of your salary into an investment account that grows tax free for you until you reach retirement age. You might be able to add money of your own to this account as well.

In some company sponsored plans, you must first put a percent of your salary into the plan then your employer matches a percent of your deposit. For example, if you put $50.00 a month into the plan, your employer might put in $25. In some companies there might be what's called a "vesting" period. That's where you must stay with the company for so many years before you can make claim on the portion the employer puts in. It's a reward system for longevity.

A young employee is frequently only concerned with how much money he/she can put into their pocket at the end of the week. However, the important thing to realize is that a single dollar, the cost of a can of Pepsi, put away today at age twenty and allowed to grow tax free, is not really a dollar, but can be much more forty five years later. The time it takes for money to double in value is approximately seventy two divided by the interest rate assuming the interest is left to compound. So, at 6%, money doubles in twelve years. At 10% it will double in 7.2 years.

Holiday, Vacation, and Sick Days To any working person, the amount of paid time off is of great interest. Federal labor laws set the minimum number of holiday and vacation days the employer must offer, depending on the size and nature of the company, but each place of business is free to offer more days above the minimum.

Paid sick days are another issue. Sick days are not mandated by labor law. If your employer offers sick days, it is out of generosity and concern for his employees. Sick days should not be considered as anything other than for sickness of the employee or a close family member unless the company policy establishes a wider guideline. Some employers may pay for some or all unused sick days at the end of the year as a reward for not taking time off. Beware: abuse of paid sick days in some cases may be grounds for the employer to eliminate this benefit.

Educational Benefits This can be a big benefit to some people. Some companies will pay for furthering your education. I know someone who got their bachelor's degree paid by their employer. Then when they graduated with a degree in computer science, the employer did not have a position open in their specialty, so they took a job with someone else. Besides the above benefits, there are other possible benefits.

Loan Repayment Some jobs, especially government type jobs, offer a loan repayment plan for paying off those huge college loans. The military, public health, and Indian Health Service come to mind.

Job Satisfaction Even when the money is good, if you don't like the work, you can't get paid enough to do some jobs. Money is not everything. Many people have given up large salaries for a lesser job with more satisfaction. For the long term, job satisfaction is very important. Included in this category might be how well you get along with the boss and other employees, if you are being challenged and not stuck in a boring routine, if you feel your work is valuable, and if you feel appreciated.

Some people however are always looking for a pat on the back, a bonus, or reward. I've been accused of being old fashioned, but my feeling is that if you haven't been fired and you continue to draw your salary… then you must be doing an acceptable job. You were hired to do a job and you did it. Why do you expect to get rewards and bonuses for doing what you are being paid to do in the first place?

Opportunities for Advancement Some jobs go absolutely nowhere no matter how long you work there while others have a clearly defined career ladder. While this consideration may be less important to a teenager looking for a quick summer job, the possibility of advancement can be very important to the new college graduate.

Miscellaneous Under this heading I include a number of intangible considerations. Sometimes they may bear more heavily than salary and benefits.

- Does the job give you valuable educational benefits or experience?
- Does the job look good on your resume?
- Would you be working with a renowned expert in your field of interest?
- Is there a chance that taking an internship would open the door to employment after graduation?

The point is: There are many, many considerations to keep in mind when looking for and deciding on a job. Salary, while often a big one, is only one consideration. But, as we find ourselves in different life situations, one consideration may outweigh others when deciding which job to take in the future.

Employee Expectations:
- To be treated equally and fairly according to all the laws and regulations pertaining to your industry.
- To be treated equal to other employees of same job and tenure.
- To get your pay accurately computed.
- To be paid on time.
- To work in a safe environment.

Employer Expectations:
- That you give him an hour's work for an hour's pay.
- Be ready to work, take breaks, lunch, and go home at the appointed times. (Coming early and staying late doesn't hurt.)
- Do the job hired to do to the best of one's ability.
- Report for work when scheduled.

Last Minute Notes:

- A job can be both pain and pleasure… often at the same time. There is rarely "the perfect job." There is always a better place to work. There will always be people that cause you major headaches, are incompetent, or shirk their duties. These are givens! On the other hand, you will often feel under-appreciated, under-paid, and that you do more than anyone else. These are also givens.

- During your employment, if your immediate supervisor should leave or be transferred, try to get that person to write you a letter commenting on your work. Keep these letters in a file for your entire employment career.

- You should always try to leave a job only when you have something else to go to. Yes, I know, you get hot and you quit in a huff. It's real macho… Don't do it! Illogical as it sounds, it is easier to find a job if you already have one.

- Always try to leave a job with good feelings between you and your employer. Sometimes this is not possible, but try. If you find yourself disenchanted with your employer, it is good to have a good honest airing out of your differences, and if it comes to the point where you want to look for a new job, be up front about it. Don't leave without giving proper notice… usually two weeks for most jobs.

- Don't burn your bridges. There are no insignificant jobs. You never know when that recommendation from the fast food place you worked at as a teenager won't help you get the better job later on. You never know when that irritating person next to you might be able to help you in a few years. Here's a nightmare…that irritating person next to you turns out to be your boss in a few years at some other company. I've seen it happen.

- When leaving a job over a disagreement, be certain to observe the company Policies and Procedures for settling disputes. It could make a difference whether or not you would qualify for unemployment benefits.

- Remember this… nothing you learn or experience will ever be wasted. The fact of the matter is, at your age, you don't have a clue what is coming in your future. Ask people you know, who are five to ten years post high school, what their lives are now versus what they had thought it would be as seniors in high school. Everyone should have a Plan A, but it is better to have a Plan B or C. And, even then… well, enjoy the ride.

Chapter 7
Renting an Apartment

At some point when you plan to leave home, you will be looking for housing. It's an exciting time and a major step. Your first apartment might be a college dorm, but it could be an apartment in a multi-family dwelling or perhaps a large apartment building. Regardless of the housing you are considering, there are many pitfalls if you don't follow some advice.

The rental of an apartment of any kind is a contract between you and the owner of the property. The owner (landlord) wants to guarantee that he will get a return on his investment and that his property will not be destroyed beyond "normal" wear and tear. You want to get value for your money and be able to live in a reasonably clean environment.

The lease, also called a rental agreement, that you will be expected to sign, will be prepared by the landlord and is written in his favor. However, it can be changed by mutual consent. The terms of the lease may be quite detailed as a result of his experience with previous tenants.

But, before you get to the lease stage, you will do a search for available apartments and then go to see the ones that you are interested in. You should generally not spend more than 30% of your take home salary on rent. This can vary depending on your needs and circumstances, but it is at least a guideline.

A landlord, according to law, cannot refuse to rent to you because of

- your race or color
- nationality
- your sex

- religion
- physical disability
- marital status

There are many, many conditions of occupancy that you must clearly understand before you sign a lease, AND must be clearly defined in the lease. For example:

- What's the monthly amount of rent and terms of payment?
- How much security deposit is required, and how many month's rent in advance? Sometimes first and last month's rent plus security deposit are required.
- What's the term of the lease? Most leases are for one year, but can be less, or more.
- What utilities are included and who pays?
- What are the rules of conduct?
- Are pets allowed?
- Can you bring in a friend with you to share the cost? If so, the friend's name should be included on the lease. How many people can live there?
- How long can someone come to visit?
- Can you sublet? Suppose the lease is for a year and, after 6 months you need to leave. Can you sublet to someone else? If so, under what conditions will the landlord allow you to do so?
- Where's the parking? How many vehicles?
- Is there a storage area?
- What's the policy for terminating the lease? Usually, after one year, the lease goes from month to month, but in any case, the landlord wants at least 30 to 60 day written notice of your intent. After all, he wants to have time to find another tenant.

If you are interested in pursuing this property, now it is time to have a good, close look at the apartment itself. The landlord himself, or his representative, will accompany you. Don't be shy. Don't hesitate to open cabinets, turn on water faucets, flush toilets, open and close doors and windows. Here's some pointers:

Bathrooms
- Is there any mold on tiles anywhere in the bathroom

(particularly the shower)?
- Is the sink enamel scratched or chipped?
- Flush the toilet and listen for any leaking sounds or other problems.
- Is there moisture or water leaking on the floor around the toilet?
- Are there any leaks in the water pipes below the sink? Be sure to check in the cabinet under the sink.
- Are faucets in working condition? Are there any leaks?

Bedrooms
- Are any shelves broken?
- Are any broken clothes hanger poles in the closets?
- Are there any mold or mildew odors in the closets?

Interior items (applies to all rooms)
- Is there cracked plaster or holes on any of the walls or ceilings? (Walls are rarely made of concrete, but rather of drywall or plaster and therefore crack easily with settling of the building.)
- Are any of the lighting fixtures broken?
- Are the carpets dirty and/or worn?
- Are there any torn draperies or broken blinds?
- If there are any ceiling fans, are they in working condition?
- Are the electrical outlets in working condition?
- Are there any roach or mouse droppings in the closets or elsewhere?

Kitchen appliances
- What appliances stay? Often the stove, refrigerator, washer, dryer, and dishwasher stay.
- Do they all work?
- Are there any leaks in the gas line for the stove?
- Inspect the refrigerator, heater, air conditioner, dishwasher, garbage disposal (in the kitchen sink; there will be an electric switch to turn it on), and faucets and make sure all are in working condition.
- Are there any mouse or roach droppings in the kitchen cabinets or elsewhere?

Security

- Are the doors leading to the outside sturdy? Is there any evidence of attempted break-ins?
- Do the deadbolts work properly? Are they loose at all? Are you allowed to install additional deadbolts on your own?
- Do the windows close and lock properly? Are there any obvious leaks that can cause cold air to come in or heat go out?
- Is all exterior lighting working?
- Is there a security code needed to get into the apartment or into the complex? If so, make sure to get those codes and remote controls, if any.

OK, here's the important part... make certain the landlord knows of any problems you see and have them written on the lease and if he promises to have things fixed before, or after, you move in, put it in writing. Another thing... **take pictures** before you move in and when you move out. Some unscrupulous landlords make a little extra money by withholding your security deposit under the pretense that you damaged the property. Get every promise in writing.

When you have nailed down all of the conditions of occupancy and you have done a thorough inspection and you have it all down on paper, you can go ahead and sign the lease and write your check. Enjoy your new freedom.

Don't forget to get renter's insurance. If you rent your home, having insurance protection for yourself and your possessions is still important. Similar to home insurance, renters insurance protects you in situations that everyone can face: fire, theft, water damage and other unforeseen circumstances your landlord's policy doesn't cover.

Renters insurance typically provides coverage, up to the limits you select, for specified items and situations, including:

- Personal property (furniture, electronics, computer equipment, clothing, etc.)
- Personal liability if someone is hurt, whether in your home or away from it
- Damage to your apartment or home caused by a covered loss

IMPORTANT: If you pay your rent with a check, write "Rent-May" in the Memo line. If, for some reason, your landlord wants cash, **insist** on a receipt.

Each choice we make causes a ripple effect in our lives. When things happen to us, it is the reaction we choose that can create the difference between the sorrows of our past and the joy in our future.
— *Chelle Thompson, Editor of Inspiration Line*

Chapter 8
Buying a House

Buying a house is a step above renting an apartment. Many of the pointers for renting an apartment apply to buying a house, just a little more involved. For example, now that you are contemplating buying, you should be interested in the age of the house and many of the core systems like the roof, heating/air conditioning system, hot water heater. In other words, you should know what you are buying. Besides your personal inspection, there are two other aids.

First, is the Seller's Disclosure Statement. This is a detailed list of all of the major issues of the residence that is filled out by the seller. It covers everything from the roof to the basement floor. This is a good starting point.

After a good thorough inspection, and you are serious, this is the time for making an initial offer and giving the real estate agent what is called "hand money" or a deposit. Often times, the buyer will make an offer about 15% to 20% lower than the asking price. Often, the seller will make a counter offer, and the negotiations go back and forth until both parties are happy.

You should be aware that the agent is the seller's agent. Although he/she may be very friendly and nice, the agent is working on behalf of the seller and wants to get the best price (the commission is based upon the final sales price). You can, at no extra charge get your own agent who will negotiate on your behalf.

The second aid, once you have come to a price agreement, is the Building Inspection Report prepared by a licensed home inspector. This is an inspection of the physical house as well as for pest and vermin. Some places also require a radon test. This is done at your expense. Choose your own inspector, not the homeowner's or the real estate agent's.

After you've seen the inspector's report, you can enter into a second round of price negotiations. If there are some things on the disclosure statement or the home inspection report that bother you, you can ask the seller to make the necessary repairs or make adjustments to the price. If there are some serious problems, you can ask that your deposit money be returned and back out of the deal. This can be heart breaking, but it is part of the process. One of the most serious complaints might be an issue of moisture or water.

When you are satisfied and ready to complete the deal, you will sign a commitment agreement, but make sure that the sale will be contingent upon your ability to get a mortgage. Like buying a car, it's good advice to be pre-approved at your bank for a mortgage. This can prevent a lot of problems.

Getting a mortgage can be another shopping experience for you. Different banks (including credit unions) will have different interest rates, terms and conditions, etc.. Go back to Chapter 2 for a refresher.

Getting pre-approved means that you will get a commitment from your bank for the amount of money they will lend, how much down payment will be required, the interest rate, terms and conditions, and any other costs involved. Sometimes they may charge points. Make sure that you can pre-pay without penalty, and that any extra money above and beyond the mortgage payment goes to the principal and not the interest. By paying off your mortgage ahead of time, you can save a lot of money, I mean a lot of money.

From this point on it just takes time. The bank has to prepare the mortgage papers, the utility companies have to be contacted to get final bills, the tax office has to be contacted, a title company is hired to check the title and to issue title insurance, and several other legal services performed. This time is also used by the buyer and seller to settle issues at their current and new residences.

Eventually, you will "close" on the house. Usually, immediately before the closing event, you should insist on a last minute walk through of the house. Make certain that all repairs or changes have been performed. If not, get it in writing that they will be. I personally know of a buyer who did not have a last minute walk through. It had rained the evening before and the beautifully finished basement had been flooded. Too late!

At the closing event, the buyer and seller meet at the real estate office where documents are signed and money exchanged. The real estate company will have prepared a "Settlement" document. This document will list what you may owe the seller and what the seller may owe to you. Be prepared to be shocked at the extra cost of settlement.

Talent is God given. Be humble.
Fame is man-given. Be grateful.
Conceit is self-given. Be careful.
John Robert Wooden

Chapter 9
Retirement

Retirement? That's so far away. I've got too many financial problems right now. I can't possibly plan for retirement. Well, yes you can, and you must. Here's some basic information to help you get started.

Many companies have retirement plans into which you put a portion of your salary. The beauty is that you don't see the money. You won't miss it. In some cases the employer will also make a contribution into the plan. THIS IS TAX FREE MONEY. This is what is called a 401k plan. If you don't participate in a 401k plan, you will be turning down free money… the money your employer contributes to match some of your contribution. So, it is free two ways, tax free and free… like in gift money.

If you don't have an employer plan, you can open up an IRA (Individual Retirement Account).

There are three types of IRA's: Traditional, Roth, and myRA. Each has eligibility restrictions based on your income, age, or employment status. The main difference is when you pay income taxes on the money you've put into the plans. With a Traditional IRA, you pay the taxes on the back end… when you turn 70½ and must take the money out as a RMD. (The Required Mandatory Distribution amount you must take out every year after age 70½ is based upon a formula using your age and the total value of the IRA as of December 31st of the previous year.)

With a Roth IRA, it's the exact opposite. You pay the taxes on the front end, but there are no taxes on the back end. And remember, in all IRA plans, your money grows tax free while it's in the account.

In the new myRA, contributions can only go into U.S. Treasury retirement savings bonds. Once the total value gets to $15,000, you must roll it over into a regular Roth IRA. Go to *myra.treasury.gov* for more information.

You can open up an IRA account at banks and investment companies. Both types of IRA are basically a savings account with big tax breaks, making it an ideal way to sock away cash for your retirement. A lot of people mistakenly think an IRA itself is an investment, but it's just a place where you keep stocks, bonds, mutual funds and other assets.

There are other differences too. While almost anyone with earned income can contribute to a traditional IRA, there are income limits for contributing to a Roth IRA. So not everyone can take advantage of them. Roth IRAs are more flexible if you need to withdraw some of the money early.

With a Roth IRA, you can leave the money in for as long as you want, letting it grow and grow as you get older and older. With a Traditional IRA, by contrast, you must start withdrawing the money by the time you reach age $70\frac{1}{2}$.

The government limits the amount you can put into an IRA each year. Most people under 50 can contribute up to $5,500 a year. That limit rises to $6,500 if you're over 50.

Selecting the kinds of investments you make with an IRA requires careful thought. Investing in CDs at your bank is the simplest and safest investment and sometimes banks charge no fees if you do this, but the return is very low.

The next step up is to invest in mutual funds. These are professionally managed portfolios of securities that you invest in, which typically offer the chance of higher rates of return. Securities of any kind, whether they are stocks, bonds or both, also carry a higher risk of loss than simple bank accounts. Before you invest, check out the mutual fund's record and read the fund's prospectus carefully to make sure that you understand what types of securities the fund invests in, and what kinds of risks and potential benefits may be associated with them. A third popular option is to choose your own stocks and other investments. Be sure you learn how the markets work and research any investment thoroughly before you commit your money.

There are many investment companies to check out such as Vanguard, Fidelity, T. Rowe Price, and Dreyfus to name a few. All of these companies have web sites with helpful information and investment plans. Your plan should be balanced and diversified. The younger you are, the more risk you can tolerate so your portfolio might be heavier on stocks and mutual funds, but as you get closer to retirement, your portfolio might lean heavier on bonds.

Before opening an IRA , get some advice. Like I've said, there are some income, age, and employment restrictions for each type.

To check out your broker, financial professional, or to get advice on scams: *www.smartcheck.cftc.gov*

I've missed more than 9000 shots in my career. I've lost almost 300 games. Twenty six times I've been trusted to take the game winning shot and missed. I've failed over and over and over again in my life. And that is why I succeed.
Michael Jordon

Chapter 10
Final Thoughts

OK, officially the book is over. Now I want to add a few important lessons that I've learned over the years that I will share with you personally. Some may sound old fashioned. That's OK. Like I sometimes say, "Some lessons come easy... some lessons come hard." Every morning on my way to school, I used to stop to pick up Alan, my friend. Every morning Alan would be late so I had to sit in his mother's kitchen and read a plaque on the wall that read, "To soon old, too late smart." You know, it took me almost 20 years to figure out what that saying meant. Here's my advice:

1. Go to your church, synagogue, or temple. Get involved, make friends, and study. If you look in on most congregations you see mostly older people. Some say that's because old people are more aware of their mortality and are afraid of dying... more sooner than later. On the other hand, the argument can be made that older people have come to realize how important church membership is. In fact, they aren't afraid of dying at all.

2. Value your friends, family, and acquaintances. In hard times, and there will be some of those, you will need them. It's been proven that people with good friends, family, and an active social life live longer, happier lives.

3. Lead a decent, honorable life. Love your spouse and cherish your kids. Money is not everything. Money does not bring success and success does not bring happiness. Divorce can be one of the most devastating emotional and financial blows to anyone's life.

4. Develop a list of business people you can trust from mechanic to grocer to banker. I've never gone into a friend's business to get

something for free. The most valuable thing was the good honest advice they might give me. Businesses have rules and then they have rules. Friends can sometimes bend them.

5. Take care of each other. For the most part, each person is in his/her own little world and, in his/her own way, facing the same problems you are. Many problems arise from honest disagreements and misunderstandings.

6. Learn to detect the warning signs that you might be dealing with someone unscrupulous. Stay alert, but not paranoid. Out of 10 people you deal with today, maybe 2-3 might not be so nice, but if you treat everyone as though they were crooks, you'd offend 7-8 of them.

7. Don't compromise with the bad ones. Turn them out immediately. One day I was shopping around several print shops for business cards. I'd standardized what I wanted so that I could compare apples with apples. Four of the shops quoted me a price in the range of $100 to $110. A fifth shop however gave me an estimate of $250. When I started out the door with a look on my face that revealed my feelings, the shopkeeper asked, "What do you want to pay?" I replied, "When I walked through that door you had a choice: to give me a fair price or to cheat me. You made the decision to try to cheat me. I won't give you a second chance."

8. There's a saying, "Follow the money." When getting advice of any kind, ask yourself, "What does this person have to gain? What does this person get out of it?" A general, but not absolute rule of thumb can be, "If the person gains anything (especially monetary) from the advice, check it twice."

Several years ago I wanted to find out how many miles I should go before getting an oil change on my car. I called Hertz, Avis, and Budget auto rental companies. I also called a cab company. My logic being that these folks deal with thousands of cars and want to keep their vehicles in tip-top shape.

Then I called one of those 20 minute lube places and checked recommendations from an oil company. Guess what I found? The car rental places and the cab companies said that they scheduled oil changes every 5-6,000 miles. The oil company said every 3,000 miles, and the lube place said every 2,000 miles. "Follow the money."

Resources Used to Write This Book

After seeing how my own three kids struggled in their young adult years after they left home, I wrote a letter to my grand-daughter over ten years ago when she graduated from high school. Since that time, in expectation of writing this book, I have saved hundreds of articles from the *Consumer Reports Magazine*, the Consumer Reports M*oney Advisor Newsletter*, articles from the *AARP Magazine*, the *AAA Magazine*, and have done hundreds of hours of research online in addition to visiting several banks and credit unions.

In addition, during these past ten years, I have purchased three homes, sold one home, purchased several cars, and self-directed my personal savings and investments.

During my 75 year lifetime, I have owned my own homes, an office building, two apartment buildings, ran four businesses, and have served five years in a money management capacity for a Home Owner's Association.

However, things do change. For example, as of this writing, there is movement to make sick pay mandatory and health care laws are evolving.

There is enormous information on line if you take the time to do the work, but then again, isn't that the secret to success anyway?

About the Author

Ron Dingee, DMD, MPH was born in Lynn, MA. After graduation from Lynn English High School, he joined the U.S. Air Force where he met his wife, Evelyn. He earned his doctor's degree in dental medicine and a master's degree in public health from the University of Pittsburgh with advanced studies at the University of London, School of Tropical Medicine.

He practiced dentistry in Greensburg, PA for almost 25 years during which time he volunteered his skills in Latin America, Mexico, Haiti, Zaire, and Thailand as a medical missionary. In 1991, he and his wife, Evelyn, sold their home and the dental practice to go to Bangkok, Thailand to co-manage the Bangkok Christian Guest House for four years. After Bangkok, they managed the Redwood Glen Baptist Camp and Conference Center in CA for three years then moved to Nevada to work with the Shoshone-Paiute Indians before retiring.

In retirement, Ron has written three books and several magazine articles.

Ron and Evelyn have three children and six grand children and now divide their time between southern CA and western PA. They are former members of the First Baptist Church of Greensburg, Pennsylvania.

Links to purchase Ron's books in print or ebook formats can be found at rondingee.com.

rondingee@aol.com

Other Books by Ron Dingee
Missionaary Memories

Missionary Memories is the story about a 93 year old father who experiences a serious health scare. His son, realizing that he really doesn't know him as well as he thought, is inspired to try to get to know him better and, in so doing, hears many extraordinary true stories of his father's earlier life as a part-time medical missionary that took him from his dental practice in western Pennsylvania to remote villages in western Africa, Haiti, Mexico, Latin America, and Thailand and the harrowing stories of people who are deprived of regular medical and dental care.

One especially intriguing story comes from the doctor's second trip to Vanga, Zaire. He says that he was napping until the small airplane banked to make its final approach to the landing field. Looking out the window to see the village below, he saw little thatch roofed huts, children waving, and ribbons of smoke from the cooking fires making it look like a scene right out of an old Tarzan movie. After landing, the plane had hardly come to a stop when a runner from the hospital approached, shouting, "You come quick. You come quick. Man from jungle come with big bone growing out of mouth."

The story also recounts many of the difficulties his son had dealing with his father's declining health, and the complexities of today's health care system. The son anguishes over many of the decisions he had to make until a friend, who had recently lost her husband, gives him some good advice.

Nanna (or How to Eat an Elephant)

Nanna (or How to Eat an Elephant) tells the story of two young men; one poor and black from the mountains of Appalachia, and the other wealthy and white from a suburb of Pittsburgh, Pennsylvania who, through a series of events, become roommates in college.

The story describes how, in two very different ways, their lives, after a tragedy, impacted a remote Appalachian community in West Virginia founded by runaway slaves back in the mid 1800's. The book is primarily fiction, but based upon the true missionary activities of a Baptist Church in Pennsylvania that changed the lives of the descendants of the founders forever.

This small church, located about 35 miles southeast of Pittsburgh, PA has, in the past 35 years, participated in missionary trips to Philadelphia, Ohio, Latin America, and eight trips to West Virginia. Also in that time, they supported, with prayers and money, the author's many trips to Mexico, Haiti, Zaire, Latin America, and Thailand.

Made in the USA
Coppell, TX
13 April 2021

53681617R00046